Under The Impression

Shockey Sanders

Copyright © 2018 Shockey Sanders
All rights reserved.
ISBN-13: 978-1726263900
ISBN-10: 1726263908

PREFACE

Thank you to every single person referenced in these pages for hurting me to the point of inspiration.
Your words, kind or damaging, have pushed me to express these memories through art.
This book in no way is to push back the pain that was put on me, but to enlighten those who have been in my same position.
My goal in writing this was to provide an empathetic voice to the people who can not speak up about specific struggles.
I pray you take something away from hearing my stories in the form of extended metaphors.
Thank you for giving me a platform and an influence.

-SS

SEE

Accidentally stumbling upon you and the fruitful bushes surrounding, a beam of light draws me in the direction of a hedge.
You are a path undiscovered by many and free of error, but it is too far out of the way to take.
The light reaches my heart, and from there I know we are compatible.
To get to you, I would be amputating my right hand.
A life without my right hand would leave me reminded of the damage I have done every day.
Reaching for something with the right would remind the left of how incomplete existence is without a lifelong companion.
But is the love of the abundant path that will last only through adolescence, worth the disability?
I can attempt to become ambidextrous.
That is my cost.
To get to you, I would be cutting my stallion loose, never to be in my control again.
He would weep, for who is to feed him or groom his mane?
His thoughts would scramble yet he did no wrong.
The rider was just not willing to commit the time for upkeep on a piece that was purely just for show.
I then would grow jealous as he moved along without me.

That is my personal price to pay.

With these decisions made, I open my third eye, and your entry becomes in sight.

I leap in excitement, assuming my next journey is a plentiful one.

Upon entering, I come in contact with a mirror.

Instead of reflecting on my own image, it reflects the path itself.

The mirror quakes, it dulls the correct path's light and makes me question its worth.

After rumbling, it shatters into a million pieces.

I cry myself a stream and the stepping stones are the undefined shapes of the tarnished reflective glass.

With every step across the flowing obstacle that I created unknowingly, the shards of the past, press harder into the soles of my feet.

I begin to bleed and question if your lambent light that melds perfectly with mine was worth the agony.

I created this mayhem for myself, yet the surrounding beauty of your perennial greenery lifts my soul.

My mind starts to wonder, what will come out of this decision?

I run on the path, three months go by.

I am joyful and in the best state possible.

Every day, you challenge my mind and draw me in with knowledge of every imaginable subject.

I continue on the path, six months go by.

I am neutral and start to notice inconsistencies in your personality.

We argue, your fruit turns to thorns which threaten to jab
me.
You no longer invite me into perusing your mind instead,
build up a wall and draw the line at my toes.
I drag on the path, a year goes by.
My feet are growing numb from bearing all the weight
being carried on my heart and mind.
You promised me forever in a city where gusts of wind
were so weak compared to our love, that we would scoff at
their attempts to blow us abroad.
You promised to fall in love with my thoughts and
romanticize through six syllable words rolling off our
tongues.
You promised me discussions of art and music at the end
of every day; we would compare literature and read each
other our deepest fears written with jet ink.
You promised to keep me dancing like a needle pressing to
vinyl, and we were the song.
Now we reach the end, your bushes and fruits have
withered, and my heels are cracked and bleeding.
All we needed was a little more precipitation and a less
harsh terrain.
I am left with no horse, worn feet, and a right hand that
has no fruit to pick from your garden.

CHERRIES

Your fruits of the spirit are rotting and falling off the trees.
They are out of season for me.
I feel as neglected as your once bountiful bushes.
Their lack of attention and water.
They remain unkempt.
You did not want to care for them until they stopped
providing everything you wanted from their branches.
You tried to bring the rich fruit back to life when they had
expired.
The fruit, being consumed by ants and parasites from the
inside out.
You could not see it rotting initially
until enough time passed and the maggots that had
manifested underneath the skin had finally surfaced.
You ask what you could have done better, and the sun
laughs
*Focused on growing the seed before concentrating on what you longed to
get out of it.*
You dreamt of picking the cherries and parading them
around in your basket,
prideful that you finally can fill the woven space that has
been vacant your whole life.
You dreamt of a thriving garden which blessed you with
produce whenever you felt desolate inside.

Your reality became a mound of bushes
locked with a key that you threw in a drawer and prayed the
precipitation in the clouds would do the work for you.

6

You forgot about the garden.
The seeds never sprouted,
the soil never fertile,
and the fruit that once grew
you killed in your own doing.
Once every leaf had fallen, and every branch grew brittle,
you begged for its regrowth.
You drowned it in tears, but the soil was too dried up to
accept the hydration that cascaded from your eyes.
There was nothing else that could save the seeds in the
ground, being suffocated by the lifeless soil.
You wept and cursed the sky when you realized your "hard
work" was atrophied.
You rushed for an end result but was not willing to take the
journey to get there.
Therefore, your once ruby red cherries
had all been consumed
by your supercilious mouth
which set fire to the garden and burnt what was left into
ashes.

ADOLESCENCE

Secure my body in a glass container.
Make the lock invisible to the imbecilic people who can not see I was born with it there.
Make the edges seamless so it appears as if you could touch me, but visible enough for the knowledgeable to spot.
Secure me in tight enough where I can breathe, but not enough where I can fill my lungs to satisfaction.
Amplify the pressure just to the point where it is physically bearable, but not comfortable.
Heighten the volume on every negative comment made about my appearance or personality while in the container, but mute the uplifting ones.
For the ones which could bring me great joy, could dissolve the surrounding glass walls that isolate me.
Do not feed me, let me watch other indulge in the fruits of life while my stomach craves what they have.
Watch me grow jealous as my body withers.
They bite their juicy peaches and consume grapes from a vine as I sit and snack on my own despair.
Let me watch as they are warm, draped in cotton and silks, spit from the highest of classes.

I am cold, my skin is bare, and I have been shaven clean to feel every gust of frigid wind that dances over my body's surface.Fixate my eyes on everyone in love, but me, capable of affection but never willing to open up when the time approaches.

Allow me to love but punish me with the reality of infidelity and dishonesty.
Break my heart piece by piece but grant it no way of healing.
Cause me to become so pulverized, not even the most skilled craftsman could repair me.
I ask all of this to make me pure.
To be broken is to be pellucid, so bring on the panes of glass that will surround me.
Let me suffer, for nothing is worse than ignorance of emotions.

SEPTEMBER

Mourn the loss of the version of me that would make sure
you had no negative feelings toward me.
The one who would be the first to make things right in the
end; who could never let you go to bed upset or angry.
Taking the blame for every scenario out of love but also
for fear of your loss.
Mourn the loss of the genuine smile seen by others that I
used to carry on my face.
The smile that people knew for being present every hour
of the day.
The pearls that would peak through soft lips, lying under
rosy cheeks and hazel eyes.
That never failed to spread its epidemic from person to
person through conversation.
Mourn the loss of the mind that could astonish yours even
after two years of its presence.
The mind that could pick yours and introduce you to
unique visions about any subject.
The thoughts that kept you up at night, being dissected one
word at a time, and adoring every minute of it.
The knowledge that you fell in love with before you ever
even knew.
Mourn the loss of the negative.
The abundance of care given to you independently, for a
small price of loyalty which you could never provide.
The fortunate loss of your demeaning statements that
blanketed my mind and soiled my positive thoughts.

The controlling nature of your words, spilling out of your
mouth like a lake after a night of rain.
Mourn the loss of the forgotten future we had planned.
With the apartment, we could just barely afford.
We were so perfect together, sharing the same final
destinations and aspirations.
See that window right there? We have a lake view, it'll be so perfect.
Just two children in love, working our way through college
for occupations to benefit us later in life.
Mourn the loss of the version of me, that loved you.
Mourn the loss of the version of me, that loved myself.

JASON'S TALE

My life is constructed of a Greek tale, a rock, and a hard place.
Where I am Jason and both detrimental choices.
The unexpected attack of all my vices catching up to me at once lingers in the back of my mind as a sip from a bottle of self deprivation.
The idea of being accosted by the scenarios I fear, haunt me while I rest.
Something I must confront but can not muster up the courage to do.
Issues that seem minuscule at surface level plunge into a dark abyss under the calm sea.
A smile that masks the more profound pain, lying behind the lens of my pupils.
There is so much I have to camouflage, yet so much I have to offer.
My life is published like Greek mythology, seen by all and unnecessarily idealized.

OPEN LETTER

I have flown up to the city twice in a month now.
I remember the first time I came up with you.
We were so young, and you had just gotten me a ring.
It did not fit and kept slipping off my finger; we would
spend hours frantically retracing our steps.
We had the trip planned to make it ideal for the both of us,
but mainly you.
Walking down 5th Avenue at eleven at night and it started
to snow, you admired me so much.
Snow started to rest on my nose and dance through my
hair, and you kissed me.
You kissed me so hard.
Your hands on both sides of my face, kissing me like it
would be the final time you would ever feel me.
You look so beautiful.
I looked so beautiful.
I started to shiver after the snow had begun to dissolve
from the warmth of my fair skin, melting away into a sheet
of frigid water that sent chills down my spine.
You gave me your jacket when all you had under was a
short sleeve top.
You were willing to obtain the bare minimum so I could be
comfortable.
We swiftly walked and held hands back to our hotel,
freezing from the wind, but internally burning with this
incredible passion we had for each other.
We laughed and joked like old souls, as our memory lead us
through the streets in the right direction.

Now, I can not remember if that scenario was a scene in a movie or the night of November 18th, 2016.
The built-up anger has ignited a new fire in me, and it is one of rage and distrust for any man to come.
What are you doing now?
What do you dream about?
Do you still have this same furry because your ideal future was given away for unexplained reasons?
Do you remember when we drove at two in the morning, exhausted from a night of dancing, and you grabbed my hand?
With tears in your eyes, you turned and looked at me and told me I was the one you wanted to spend the rest of your life with?
Do you remember the genuine feeling of companionship we felt, more than a couple, but as absolute best friends?
Do you still foresee the day we would have collected enough money to pay for the down payment on our city brownstone?
Or was all of that just in the movie plot I have romanticized?

Under The Impression

IT'S ALL I HAVE THOUGHT ABOUT FOR FIVE MONTHS

In your passenger seat,
I am so comfortable with you.
We drift to a bigger city in your sports car.
You go 90 in a 55, and it is my form of entertainment
seeing you get an adrenaline rush.
It was my day to do whatever I desired, and I chose exactly
what you enjoyed as well.
Our favorite album playing during our long drive to a
vintage record shop.
Talking about anything and everything,
you were my everything and anything.
My best friend at first,
then someone I slowly grew to adore,
even if I never vocalized it.
I used to sit next to you in your car admiring your chiseled
face and letting my fingers explore your thick curls.
Now I sit alone, feeling tears flow down my cheeks and
chopping inches of my long hair off the every time you
hurt me again by not being by my side.
This is it?
I return your clothes and pretend like you are not what
keeps me up at night? I spend my days recalling your smell
and missing your voice. You are probably sleeping sound at
the moment while I lie awake restless,
releasing all the things I can not tell you onto a white page.
You have become deaf to my pain.
Call it the inability to process how much I miss you or call
it selective hearing.

Either way, you do not care to concern yourself with my
sanity. Oh, what a straightforward message from you could
do to me in this moment.
Then I come to realize,
the tables have made a turn,
I now experience the pain I was deaf to when you felt it.
I then come to realize,
I deserve it all.
Every tear spilling from my ducts is one that I brought
upon myself.
In your words, it's all I have been thinking about for five
months.

DEFROST

Having slow-motion flashbacks like an old black and white film.
My unwelcoming heart begins to soften, and I experience a flutter in my stomach and head.
A wave of euphoria does not even compare to the rush I get from recalling the way your eyes gazed into mine at red lights.
Your trivial smirk that was born from all of the one-liners I memorized to make you laugh like a child.
My vast smile anytime you would grab my left hand and steer with your knee.
This exposition of our vintage love story set the scene for two people so infatuated with each other, but never willing to disclose it.
I miss the way you read me so well.
The way a singular comforting embrace from you could rearrange my disposition for the day.
You departed so quickly.
We could have made minutes into months.
Instead, you lasted a lifetime, but only a fall season to the world.

IN SECRET

My heart rate exceeds the average beats per minute.
I am overwhelmed with this blitz of exuberance and
lustfulness.
I am satisfied just sitting with you, allocating all of our
opinions
on music and art.
Have you heard this song? It reminds me of you.
You open my mind to new topics and theories to explore.
I have never felt such warmth radiating from one's soul.
You did not even have to touch my skin for my body to
absorb your loving energy.
I missed so much about you.
I would cry at your absence.
Now you sit next to me as the sky paints a masterpiece.
You sit and admire the way the clouds intermingle with
pink air.
My eyes are fixated on your subtle jaw line; I take deep
breaths of your musk that used to linger on all my clothes.
A wave crashes on the beach such as a stream of content
washes up on my body.

Under The Impression

DO NOT READ

The cold tile of my bathroom floor is chilling my nerves to
the point of desensitization.
More broken than tears can ever compensate for, I endure
a sense of calm, an overwhelming, unnerving feeling.
Everything goes silent, and I stop panicking, stop shaking.
All the distress I feel on a day to day basis because of
another's actions can all just vanish.
The options and scenarios rush through my head, and the
pace of my thoughts pick up again.
I'm in fight or flight mode.
My body's adrenaline goes into overdrive, making
everything move faster than before.
Nothing but the absence of pain or emotion and the sound
of my pulse as it pounds through my fingertips.
I start to breathe deeply, dry cry and back myself into the
corner of my all white bathroom.
Gripping the phone in my hand, I'm clutching it like it is
my only possession.
Plotting to discard the device that was used to tarnish my
name and breaking it to the point of uselessness;
I beam the pointless piece of glass at the shower wall, it
shatters.
Its fragile body is destroyed, and still, that phone was
stronger than I am.
The impression and blunt finale of this night remain
unfinished.

NOW IN THEATERS

Falling in love with a stranger, a stereotypical movie plot.
I live in a film with a convoluted meaning of attraction.
Every day I wake up with a new story to relay.
Obtaining a heart that cares too much, wanting to give everyone compassion, takes a critical toll.
I have a heart that lives in a world where monogamy is glorified and breaking detailed rules from thousands of years ago is frowned upon.
I am expected to find one person, a singular being, and share every thought, feeling, and emotion with them until my physical body can not withstand daily trials and tribulations.
There is no possible way that someone is out there, with all the characteristics that perfectly match my profile.
I have, what, twenty years left if I am lucky to find this person before my body finally takes its last breath?
This person who will tolerate me expelling utter nonsense about music or art or my opinions.
Someone to relate to and care for and put before me in many aspects. This person is just a dream to me, not a reality.
Just because I am young does not mean that it is too early to recognize what I want for my future.
The world enjoys tossing titles at people like me, I rebuke these titles.
I do not need a combination of letters and Latin roots to justify my feelings for others or my view on love.

RADIO SILENCE

I am waiting for that
It hurt to see you text.
The one where you tell me that you forgot how my laugh
sounds and how much you missed it.
I did not get a hello, not a hug, not a smile.
I got shallow looks and side eyes while you tried not to be
bothered by my presence.
I know you, I know that there was only one thing on your
mind all night.
Catch a glimpse before I get caught staring back at you,
then look back at your phone and continue to entertain the
next girl you think could top me.
Pretend like every emotion did not come back when you
walked through that door and was surprised by my
attendance. I could not even place your voice, its absence
from my life since February. Tell me you missed me, tell me
you hated seeing me, tell me I made you cry. Anything. I
need to hear something. Reach out to me and confirm that
the longing feeling in my heart is not an independent one.
You look so different, but your lips are still the familiar
ones I used to kiss. When I look at you, no longer do I
visualize the hurt. I see the repentance in your eyes and
connect that to the same way ours would lock while having
introspective conversations. Yours, almost always
bloodshot due to your vices and mine always welled up due
to my routine ways.
My stomach drops every time a buzz comes from my
phone, it is still not your name.

RERUN

I wish I could slow down certain moments in time just
to feel specific emotions one more time in my life.

The rain on your windshield, the faint tapping sound as
the drops splatter on the glass.
How the bright red signal spread its rays through the wet
surface, generating a glow.
The warmth of your hand on mine as you rub your
thumb on the back of my palm.
My eyes burned, trying to stay awake and right as I was
about to drift of,
Shockey
I shot awake to hear your monologue about how our last
three months have changed you.
My heart started to race as I knew what was coming and
I was aware my life would be revised from that moment on.
Immature love makes your heart levitate, leave your
body.
You are told you are loved, and you want to jump up and
down, you want to sob, and if it is not your first time, you
see the end.
That perfect scene, one that was quintessential enough
to be in a movie, will be engraved in my thoughts for them
as long as I have a heartbeat.

FRENCH GUADELOUPE, '16

I wish I could analyze the stars for the rest of my life.
Gazing up into a dark sky and having no worries, feeling
weightless.
Capturing the moments with my eyes in complete
silence as my mind flows freely about anything and
everything.
The sound of the ocean and the white noise of nature
manufactured a smile, I felt so minuscule.
Though at this time I was not as deteriorated as I am
now, I felt as if all of my problems melted away.
I gained a new perspective on what should be affecting
me on a daily basis and what should only last in my mind
for a couple seconds.
I thank the world for these situations, I curse the world
for having me not experience them since.

HOW COULD I HAVE FORGOTTEN?

I recount the time we spent together, everything was so pure and lighthearted.
My inability to speak with an uninfluenced mind directs me in the way of deceit and isolation.
My mistakes reflect my rigid past, which affect my choices in the future.
The amount of damage I did to you did not call for the actions you did unto me.
Now it is more than a few months later, you are back to clear things up.
Conversation flows, I miss you.
We start to catch up on simple topics, I long for you.
I go in depth of how empty I have been without you, I need you.
I wish things could be different
A sentence of a coward, make it different, make it work with me.
Do not break my heart again for revenge.
You felt as broken and lonely as I did the night we called it off, I just wanted to hold you again.
The loss of you from my life and the death of the future we planned step by step every day.
Just pretend like we never had a perfectly executed escape to finally be happy together.
We would never be one again anyway, right?
We're still sticking to our plan.
We're gonna reconnect years from now, talk over a nice sit-down dinner, and fall in love.

My heart drops, recalling the first time we had this
conversation.
We're still gonna get married Shockey, ha, you thought I forgot?
You always know how to make me stop crying, but in
the timing of this, you intensified the tears.
As much as I wanted to believe that you cared, I
wondered how many other girls you also have under this
impression.

STANDARDS

The inability to open up has sent me back to my dark room, locking every door.
My incapability of retaining feelings, negates the positive surrounding me.
The hurt that changed me forever on a night in June still curses me with its noxious cloud over my life.
Looking back, the split itself does not linger, the shadow cast over my mentality and heart is what stays.
The tangible feeling of my emotions being covered in a thick, black tar that immediately dried and has not cracked since. The tunnel vision of never finding another that holds my interest and keeps me smiling seems to always be consuming my thoughts.
This overcoming pressure to find another who has the same physical attributes, family privilege, and intelligence as I do is saddening.
What if all I want is someone in my life who can make me genuinely smile?
Someone who I can actually stand by and be proud of, not because of a dollar amount, but because of how they have brought me back to life. Does no one understand how desperate I am to have love? I have everything handed to me in life, but the one thing I want the most is something that I will never be able to give myself.
All the money in the world, all the extravagant gifts, all the boys who drive custom cars, none of that could make me confident enough to step off the ledge to loving someone or myself again.

QUESTIONS I WOULD ASK IF YOU SPOKE TO ME

Why do you act like seeing me didn't kill you inside?

Why do you keep coming back into my life just to hurt me and leave it again?

Why do you not see how much I care(d) about you even after all the repeated hurt?

Why can't you realize I trusted you with so much and you threw that all away?

Do you realize you will have to see me every week?

Why do you feel the need to break me down right when you start to build things back up?

Did you even see a future with me?

What did I do to make you never want to speak to me again?

What really is "leaving the past in the past"?

ADD YOUR NAME

I have hit that wall.
One where nothing can make me wallow anymore,
doesn't the pseudo look good on me?
Indifferent, leaving every message unopened.
I have better things to do than to worry about this mess.
Keep telling yourself that, Shockey.
With a stomach too empty to throw up and a body too
dehydrated to cry, what do you resort to?
Not the ignorance of sleep, no, in fact, you will wake up
the next morning with clouded thoughts and a lingering
issue.
Not the typical nature of discussion, for that will bring
you back to the heavenly hours and fade the mundane
connection.
Take the silent route, the route of isolation.
Just to prove you truly are unbothered.
Sell it, make them all believe you could not care less or
dare to bat an eye over the loss of someone who you saw
yourself with for months to come.
Add your name to the list, right under the others who
have pushed me to insomnia and an addiction to speaking
through my laptop keyboard in the first hour of the
morning.
You have fulfilled the legacy, and the next to come will
hear your name on the list of those who have hurt me.

THE ENDS

Our time we spent together was a double negative.
You took advantage of something already distressed and
in need of help.
The midnight conversations helped the emotions but the
way you would pretend you did not have many, affected my
physical body.
A mind filled with you and a heart filled with weariness.
The lack of title and the abundance of pressure made
me take the jump to do things out of character.
You were my biggest regret, and my only covet at the
same time.
The lack-there-of relationship caused me to question
every feeling endured.
Yet the way you could coax me into believing you could
relate to my pain kept me going back.
Why do the evilest people enjoy damaging the previously
broken?
The time where all I needed was an inspiration, you gave
me a dark path.
You lead me to a morbidly introspective state, leaving
me wetting my cheeks, sitting on the floor of my
bathroom, scared that my life was in my own hands.
My eyes are swollen because I am hurt "out of love."
No.
Love would not scar the way you did when you
attempted to help.

Under The Impression

Love would not overbear the way you did when I placed
a foot in the wrong direction.
Love would not leave me in bed, preparing to wake the
next morning with swollen eyelids and a headache.
Although you delivered your final goodbye, this will not
be the last I hear from you.

I will apply the one thing you taught me, not to reach
out again to someone who has hurt you.
You will not be hearing from me.
With your number deleted, I have no temptation.
Let me disappear, watch me have no attachment when I
leave for a month, a thousand miles away, and witness me
flourish.
By the start of next year, you will be drowning in the
apprehension, and I will be overcome with success.
My face will be a memory from a small snippet from life,
and your name is already distant from my mind.

If I am that disposable for you, then likewise.
Although this appears to be another story of heartbreak,
it is far from it.
This is the first step to recovering the respect I have lost
for myself, never again will I let another desert me the way
you have.

Under The Impression

VOLKSWAGON BUS

How infamous your name is to my existence and to any
of the ears who have heard of your actions.
You took so much of my pleasure by attempting to
provide some for yourself.
Thinking about what you stole from me no longer wells
my eyes, but makes me smile.
Look how far I have come, I am no longer the person
you hurt. I am crazy, right? I am just lying.
Try and convince yourself of that falsehood but the
emotional scars I carry do not deceive.
A handful of people recognizing the tragedy turned into
an entire county, that fact no longer worries me.
The anger you carry for yourself was passed onto me
but flourished into self-love.
What you attempted to steal, you provided.
I found what I was looking for, you are still searching.
You sought sorrow and self-condemnation and spite.
I found self-love, hope, and myself.
I could walk around a victim to the way you forcibly
lusted me.
Instead, I carry it as pride.
A pride that I am strong and have overcome what others
fear. Let me be an advocate for hope since I am brave
enough to share my story with those who could judge me.
Tell me I am lying, tell me it was my fault, yell from afar
that I was asking for it.
Believe your fabrication, and I will trust in my own
reality.

HOW ABOUT NIGHTS

How tempting it is to run away like we talked about.
The promises you once made to me that we would fall in love in the city, disappeared like the lust I had for you in my heart.
Yet every time you look at me with those squinted brown eyes through your glasses, I forget the continuous anguish you caused me to endure.
When I hear your voice, I can not remember the times you made me cry. I do not want to think back to those moments, for I can not manufacture ill thoughts toward you.
Picture this
You whisper with such excitement,
You'll go to class, and I can wait for you at the apartment.
I'll wait for you.
My heart flutters, every emotion comes back.
Love, anger, sadness, longing, hate, compassion, empathy. I want to cry, but I want you to stop deceiving me. I have missed you even though you have tarnished my ability to love and I walk back into the exposure of hurt once again. It feels so right that I do not care if pain occurs, it will be worth it. We are just kids, and we do not mean any of this nonsense. Let me convince myself of that when I know all my manipulated mind wants is to be with you forever and have things unfold as planned.
Once we were so infatuated with each other, now I see you one day a week and pretend we no longer speak.

Under The Impression
HE LEANED IN TO KISS ME AND SAID

I have thought about you every day since we last talked.
Letting you leave my life is my biggest regret, I know I pushed you out of it.
I miss talking to you every day, I miss your wisdom.
You made my days bright, and I felt as if we make such a great pair.
Forget what anybody says, if I am happy, what do they care?
This will not be a secret, I am so excited for you to be mine and for everyone to see.
We are doing what we have always felt was right.

-how your eyes continuously lie

NO HAPPY ENDING

She ties the blindfold behind her head, making sure
none of her silky hair gets caught in the knot.
A respected man has promised the woman a life
abundant with compassion and love if she can just
complete the maze.
Willingly knowing she will navigate the seemingly simple
maze with no vision, she enters with a smile.
Blinded to the danger that can crouch behind any turn,
she steps one foot at a time on the grass.
Since sight is absent, the alternative senses take control
and advise her through the perennial garden.
The first monster she encounters is Lust, and they
become one.
With the self-inflicted blindness placed upon her own
pupils, Lust directs the woman and offers guidance to the
prize that awaits.
Lust and the woman travel along together, and the
uplifting spirits with good intentions carry along.
The beast waiting around a lifeless hedge is Deceit, he is
a robust creature who has an influential voice.
Deceit commands that the two find a new route,
ensuring them that the path they have pursued only leads
to destruction and depression.
Lust and the woman do as Deceit says and explore
secondary ways, as the two are removed from earshot,
Deceit maniacally laughs.
Wondering which trail they should select next, Hatred
dashes in front of them.

It is all falsehood, he rushed to inform them no longer
embark on the journey, there is nothing at the end.
A creature with the name of Perseverance comes to
swallow him up, the woman does not think twice about the
encounter and Lust moves them along.
The partners can sense the prize awaiting and eagerly
rush toward the center of a rose bush.
Lifting the hood of the wooden trunk that awaited her,
she removes her blindfold.
A mirror is set facing her in the trunk, her prize she had
fought so vigorously for was herself.
She has beaten the demons and won herself back, the
companion she had lacked.
Though it was not the prize she wanted, it was the gift
she needed.

I WISH I DYED MY HAIR

I wish I made quick decisions that revealed your harsh judgment before I became involved with you.

I wish I was hasty and made spur of the moment choices that would have caused you to think of me poorly. Knowing you would become unattracted to someone slightly different than you, I wish I had dyed my hair blue.

Doing what I truly wanted, considering your detrimental view of originality, was never an option as long as you were present. I wish I could have dressed how I wanted without your insecurities being asserted unto me.

I wish I would have worn vibrant colors to make you uncomfortable with the surplus amount of ingenuity. Aware of your inability to appreciate change, I wish I had gotten the piercings I had always wanted. Making slight changes to my appearance was forbidden if you did not approve of them beforehand.

I wish I could have expressed myself through artwork and writing without being told it was unavailing. I wish you were uplifting when I acquired modish interests. The conscience of the way your love for me would shift, I wish I had cut my hair.

FOREVER AND A DAY

I could talk to you until hell freezes over
and we have only had an abrupt discussion.
Disappointed by the idea that we are incapable
of becoming more than casual acquaintances,
I will proceed to discard my feelings for you.
It is impossible for you to give me the time of day,
or if you do, I will not be able to recognize it
due to my insecurity.
You ask me about tattoos,
I question you about something
but the category slips my mind
due to how I was internally losing my composure.
That one conversation has plastered a smile on my face
since.
So I wait, wait for the next opportunity to engage in a
forgettable conversation that will romanticize our
coexistence.

NAVIGATING

There is a man who is infatuated with me, his name is West.

West loves the idea of me and the possibility of growing together until he is shipped off in nine months.

West writes to me everyday, stories of love; he can use four syllable words which is something I am not used to seeing when it comes to men.

He wishes to see me at least once a week, splitting a bottle of wine and discussing what he envisions for our partnership. I do not like West, for he moves quickly and in a direction I am not comfortable with.

He likes to take pictures of me and pin them around his room to remind him of what he strives to obtain.

I find it eerie, he finds it romantic. For I am not even his own, and he parades me like we have been married for a decade. West likes to know what makes me cry at night, he says it shows him I am capable of feeling.

West has nothing to cry about at night, except the fear I will never love him the way he loves me.

He says he has dreamt about me years ago and has prayed for me since he was young but I have been told to avoid boys who treat you like their mothers.

West is too delicate for my taste, he makes me feel too good about myself and cannot admit when I do not look impeccable.

I will never care for West, he has given me everything I look for in a rushed period of time, and I am merely disinterested.

PUPPY DOG

I obtain not trust for men until it comes it you, then it grows bountiful.
You could slap me across the face, and I would still greet you with a smile.
You can ignore me Tuesday night but have me at your feet by Wednesday.
You could break my heart, and I would apologize for deeds that I did not commit;
mending my heart back together independently.
You can push me to insanity then have me come crawling back with an empathetic heart.
You could bash my name, and I would answer with elation if you called me after.
I am disposable to you, but the minute you yearn for me again, I am still here waiting for you.
You have promised so many unfulfillable futures for us, and I believe every word that comes from your mouth.
I just stick around until the day that you no longer wish to use me, then I spend the next two months heartbroken until you decide to come around again.

"AM I WAISTING MY TIME TRYING TO LOVE YOU?"

Yes.

A REMINDER TO MYSELF ABOUT BOYS WHO POSE AS MEN

You never worry about the younger woman who
continuously rings your boyfriend's phone until she is in his
bed on Thursday after your split on Monday.
The fraudulence of his words come back to haunt your
thoughts at two in the morning as you listen to the song he
would sing to you.
Never genuinely valuing what you had with him in the
first place, a dry cry is the only performance you can put
on for yourself.
After the five months and five breakups, you two had no
chance of recovering from the shaky foundation that the
"love" was built on.
No amount of apologies force you to forget the girls he
could instigate while you two were not on speaking terms.
The girl with the long, fried blonde hair with the name
of a house pet who was nothing more to him than that.
What was her reasoning to call you the nights you slept
over?
The quiet brunette who came from a complicated family
that always seemed to be in need of a ride.
What would you two talk about when alone and driving,
or was there no talking at all?
I no longer trust men who are eight months younger
than me and play around with drugs on the weekend.
Although they are old enough to entertain a woman, it
does not mean they can keep that woman's blabbering
mouth at rest.

41

LAMENTAR

It is hard to envision what you are doing at this very moment.
Most definitely not seducing someone new, there is no one else who would tolerate your ignorance as I did.
No one who could overlook your immaturity as quickly as I did.
How did we even get involved with each other, such a mistake?
You soiled my name as I brought yours to attention.
Whatever alter ego overthrew my morals did it quickly and swiftly.
I never truly wanted to damage you but also never honestly cared enough about you to make you mine.
You would have traded happiness for me, yet I could not find joy in you for months.
Maybe this was the experience you needed to overcome your childish ways if that is even feasible.
Contact is nonexistent since you have blocked my number and I have returned the favor.
I never cared to talk to you, as you felt like a burden.
A crying child that longed for attention every hour of the day and would scream louder if it did not receive it immediately.
How annoying was the wailing child I had to tend to at the most inconvenient times?

PINK ALLIGATOR SHORTS

I once met a dog at the beach, he was soft-spoken and
wore a cap of black curly hair.
With his skinny caliber and faint muscles that peaked
through his dark skin, he carried himself with spunk.
We sat on a ragged towel until the sun was extinguished
by the water on the horizon.
He spoke about a sport he participates in that most
likely costs him thousands, but he did not seem to mind.
Born in Brazil, he spoke Portuguese and had a father
who lingered in their home country who he said never
called.
It was tranquil dawn, we exchanged numbers and went
separate ways.
As the temperature increased, so did his attraction to
me.
He would talk to me until I fell asleep and be the first
name I would see in the morning.
I later found out he was in love with a woman who he
shared a name with.
To this day she has no clue what her partner was doing
while she was sitting at home.
Who would have guessed he had enough time on his
hands to juggle a woman besides his girlfriend?
His occasional casualty of calling me another name
alarmed me, but I was always coaxed into thinking nothing
of it.At the end of our short fling, I had learned his mind
was not as bright as the fluorescent shorts that he wore
when we met.

A CONSTANT ROTATION

Sunsets used to
make me mourn.

The star being
put to rest
manufactures
such colors that
will always remain
constant.

Gradients of hues
that creates effortless
beauty to provide
hope as night
approaches.

The earth's show
that I anticipate
at dawn keeps my
days upbeat.

Sunsets bring me joy.

I WISH WE WERE IGNORANT

There was never a sober moment spent with you.
You, intoxicated out of your mind from whatever you
forced in your glass piece that morning. Me, high from the
infatuation I had for you, that was all I necessitated. While
you were alone at night, your eyes bloodshot from the
smoke, mine were overcome with tears. You forced me to
wonder if I was not suitable enough to be around while
clear headed.
The discomfort to see you not able to enjoy life lays
heavy on my heart.
With your mentality of living without regrets, you
overlooked our future.
How are we supposed to make our grand getaway if you
narcotize your existence?
The single moments I would see you smile were after
you took a hit, I felt so irrelevant to your contentment. I
rather see you fight depression with isolation than with
cowardliness like you currently do. I wish I could have
loved you before that girl with the forgettable name ruined
you. The you that was knowledgeable and could engage in
discussion on any topic.
I wish there was a version of me that did not mind the
lack of sobriety you obtained.
Instead, I sit, write, and cry; drunk off the idea of a
healthier you.

TO DO LIST:
FEBURARY 3RD, 2018

-Eat, do not forget to attempt to eat something

-Put your phone away for just a little bit, it's good for you

-Ice your eyes

-Hours of unbeneficial work

-Coffee

-Write out your day for tomorrow, get it together

-Drive over to give his shirts back

-Throw out the artwork

-Cry in the shower

READ IT AND WEAP

You are too irrelevant to write a poem about, so you get
a memoir.
One moment of your ignorance is not worth an entire
ode.
Furthermore, I repeat the story to emphasize the hurt.

You were high, you did not mean what you said when
you told me that it is upsetting to speak to me.
The single sentence spewed from your callous mouth
lead to a night of my wet face pressed into my pillow,
forcing myself to sleep.
I could notice you growing detached ever since we last
kissed.

We kissed sitting on the wet grass in the dark, while
people surrounding us danced, and ambient lights strobed.
It was just an extemporaneous kiss, a meaningless kiss.
Understandably, we do not view the instant alike.
You see a special memory that represented present
feelings and a promising future together.
I saw an opportunity to live in the past but not revive its
existence.
We were incapable of seeing our bond in a similar light.

CROSS-EYED

It is evident that you are just leading me
down a path of remorse.
You do not discuss music with me
like we once did.
You sleep until two in the afternoon
and expect me to converse with you when it is
convenient.
I only receive word from you
at one in the morning.
Such a perfect opportunity was dispatched,
I cared so deeply.
Under no conditions could you trust me
and I could not have reliance on myself.
I obtain a mind poisoned by your promises
which all include you loving me;
we know that will never happen.
You continue to attempt to deceive me,
yet I am conscious of the sin
your tongue conveys.

NUMBER ONE: NARCISSISTIC

On my phone, there is a file of
words or phrases drafted over the course of a year.

Every time I think about "him," I write down a
quality or event that bothered me in the relationship. My
list hold over
two-hundred bullet points.

Two-hundred times I have thought about you for longer
than a minute.

Two-hundred qualities
I was blinded to when under your influence.
There is no longer a purpose for me to expel any anger
or sadness unto this list.

Two-hundred bad experiences
outweigh the two-hundred thousand valuable ones.
There is no longer a purpose for me to keep the list for any
sentimental or tender reason.

RED LIGHT REMINISCENT

On my sixteenth birthday, I removed my makeup with
tears.
The tears I shed were never of joy or exuberance, always
fear.
The pejorative backlash of every action I would
innocently commit could not even cease on my birthday.
On the fifth of May, I cried until my eyes burned.
Driving with me in your passenger seat, you headed in
the direction of my home. My eyes start to well up, you
forgot what day it was.
On Christmas, I looked myself in the mirror and
realized I had a problem.
After enduring a night filled with speculations thrown at
my brittle, eighty-pound body, I starting to think the name
calling was accurate.
I was not hungry at the most inconvenient times.
On a night at the beginning of June, I imagined my life
to be over though it was just beginning.
Sitting on a rod iron chair of my hotel balcony, I hung
up the phone with no tears left to weep.
I rushed to the bathroom to throw up my dinner and my
sorrow.
I spent three hours deleting every memory, yet the ones
I wanted to scrap the most were the ones engraved in my
thoughts.
On my drive home from my "vacation," every red light
we halted for was reminding of the insults you would gift
me when we stopped for traffic signals.

WOMANLY EXPECTATIONS

I never wish to bear a child.
For what reason would I want to subject another being
to such a cruel world?
I am expected to raise them with my moral image yet, I
do not even obtain one of my own.
My role is portrayed to be a responsible figure who has
enough wisdom to relay to another.
I believe this earth is damaged and does not necessitate a
child from my own womb.
Leave the obligation to those who have a calling for
parenthood.
I will grow old with my graduate degree and a trust fund
for my brothers kin.
Spending the most glorified years of my life with heavy
eyes and disheveled hair is not appealing.
Living my years to their highest potential is in my future,
whether it be with a significant other or on my own.
I will be pushed in the direction that will be most
beneficial for me, it will be the world's way of
compensating for the ill memories.

NEVER TRUST A MAN BY HIS ABILITY TO CHARM

I was forcibly subjected to a plethora of information about you tonight.
Feeling like I was being betrayed for the third time, I withheld tears like a poorly constructed dam.
The blonde one warned me to your manipulative personality as if I had not already known.
The girl with the benevolent smile listened as I expressed the care I had obtained for your mentality.
Neither believed my name was independent to your tongue, as yours was to mine.
I had hoped to be deaf at the moment, for your image in my head was conflicting to the one in my heart.
How I wish my logical mind acquired ignorance to your mental abuse.
I no longer view your face fondly, my stomach ceases to flutter at your eyes.
Your lips, I now view as a device to flatter other women, not the pair that formerly pressed into my forehead.
I should have been attentive to my fingers, writing poems about your future deceit that manifested within the empty compliments.

TESTING THE WATERS

On a day
I expressed arbitrary courage.
I read a few drafts of pages I had written
To my family.
I exhaled after delivering the story with identical emotion
To that of which I felt while writing it.
Are you not able to write anything happy?
My mother looked at me in my tired eyes and questioned.
No,
I blatantly stated and smiled to lighten the mood.
Happy is easy. It is childs play to tell stories of exuberant love and blessings.
She always found my candid wisdom humorous.
It is more challenging to write about the minuscule thoughts that damage, but ultimately inspire.
Happy is easy, I don't like easy.

I KEEP HIS NUMBER BLOCKED BECAUSE OF

All the songs
that play while
I sit in my
pitch
black
room that remind me of him.

Yet,

no amount of
three-minute melodies
would make me miss his abuse.
His manipulation
that was sent
in the form
of a caring
friend.

DANCING AROUND REASONING

I am asked by a boy,
Why I do not trust men.
Well, I would have to trust you to answer that.
I reply,
attempting to finalize the conversation.
Not considering that statement a just answer, he pursues
me further.
How can I get you to trust me?
I tell him the process would take time and seem
impossible.
Then he asks again why I can not express my reason for
distrust.
Well, I would have to trust you to answer that.

KISS ME GOODBYE

You entice my mind with thoughts of a future outside
of this suffocating state that sends me into deep
contemplation.
It jumbles my thoughts.
Why can I not easily move on? You are psychotic and
toxic, but for some reason, my mind tells me to love you
until my heart takes a final beat.
Why do I cherish the smile that diminished mine?
The eyes that used to connect with mine, now cause my
own to weep.
I miss your touch, it came with violence.
The mental violence that caused me to be more restless
than your insomnia currently does.
Those three A.M conversations, I hope you have
dismissed them from your memory.
Everything plays out for the greater good, but your final
goodbye sent me spiraling back to square one.

ROOM 243

I have concluded that the insane find me.
Seeking help,
guidance,
or Support.
Although not tolerable, it is comfortable for a blip of
time.
One soul told me that she knows I fall asleep before her,
To watch my back and stay on good terms with her.
She used my fear of being disliked against me.
Somehow, she had known me for a short forty-eight
hours but read me better than a majority of men have.
This amount of culture division caused many issues in
our coexistence.
While I would be battling restlessness, she was shouting
at a man on the phone in the single digit hours of the
morning.
With my passive personality and my pseudo exuberance,
I wished to remain quiet.

107

Who knew that all it took was a change of location to heal my heart.
The feelings that were manufactured for you were ones of those together for seasons.
Why do we have to be separated by one thousand miles but have a synchronized spiritual connection?
We had five days yet turned them into five years.
I fell for you as fast as humanly possible in a short period.
You say we can reconnect, I will forget you by then.
You will disremember me as well, there are more beautiful girls out there.
They may be more attractive, but I doubt that could bring out integrity in you like I could.
Go back to your hometown and reiterate my name to the people who will not find the same appeal in hearing it as you do.
Possibly one day we could meet again and fall in love.
I believe, in the future, we will only recollect the number of our humorous commonality.

-forget this number

BEHIND THEIR EYES

I met a girl who outwardly is secure and content.
How does she do it?
How is she able to arise and voluntarily put on a smile
for the world to see and celebrate?

I met a girl who had limited self-worth yet was incredibly
exuberant.
How is she able to find so much happiness in things
outside of herself?
Does she ever consider the type of person she is and cry
herself to sleep?

I met a girl who had her entire life devised for her, yet
she was lost.
How did she have a clear path leading toward success
and still manage to wander on the way?
How was she accustomed to the way her parents
mistreated her?
I met a boy who was chiseled and wealthy.
How was he able to maintain an unpolluted mindset
with the demons surrounding him?
How was he able to rearrange my mindset with one
sentence about his worldly view?
I met a girl who finally was able to love herself and was
satisfied with the person she had grown to be.
It seemed so effortless to her.
Why did it take me a year journey to achieve this
mindset? Why do I still feel I have not reached the end?

HOLISTIC

I feel the lighthearted warmth from your presence
And optimism from your mind.
Coming from an individual
that has obtained a dormant heart for a year,
I feel for you.
Not in the way that I feel for
The homeless woman and child I pass
on my way to morning sessions.
This is a novel kind of euphoria.
The kind of experience you only dream about.
Like your soulmate kissing you goodbye
to go to work, and you treasure them.
You know you love them.
I am able to feel.
The adornment I have finally obtained for myself
can now be partially given to another.
I feel future and success from your name
and spirituality from your heart.
Coming from a being
who did not used to believe in a future for themselves.

DUST OFF THE BOX

The scratchy, blue fabric seats of the Red Line irritated
my thighs on my ten P.M train ride.
I am tired, more than tired, I am exhausted.
I had spent my morning crying in my dorm and my
afternoon with swollen eyes that gave away my sentiment.
My head is resting in mid-air, my eyes are shut, I am
dozing off. I can hear the people hustling out of doors
around me, but I am too fatigued to watch.
My body is cold, but my eyes feel so inflamed and hot
from the sorrow. I miss having a person that would give me
their jacket if I even so much as twitched.
I miss the soft kisses on my forehead.
The doomed feeling of not being able to obtain these
emotions again haunts my thoughts as I sit on this packed
train. At this moment, I felt a body sit next to me.
Now, this was a boy I knew, and I could tell by his
palpable kindness. He caressed my head, placed it on his
shoulder, and kissed my forehead.
I lifted my eyelids and he had his jacket is his hand,
offering it to me.
While I put the jacket on, he smiled and looked at me in
a particular adoring way.
I bundled up and placed my head back on him.
My wishes were fulfilled; unfortunately, one thousand
miles and one thousand kept secrets separate us.
He broke down my walls and helped me trust others in a
short period of time; merely an experience to adjusting to
love again.

A SATURDAY AFTERNOON IN 2021

In my dreams,
I am living in Chicago,
walking to grab some coffee with a guy I met at work.
On my walk,
I listen to my favorite sad songs.
Sad songs are my equivalent to comfort foods,
since the feeling is most familiar.
The day is seventy and sunny
with a little breeze.
I am wearing a black jean jacket that is worn
and some pants to match the climate.
Briskly walking,
I approach the coffee shop,
not nervous or timid.
My skin is warm from walking
on the side of the street that the sun hit.
I order my usual iced coffee
and sit at a table in the sun,
I am always early.
He arrives, we talk.
It is enjoyable.
We smile at each other
and hug before going separate ways.
I begin to walk home
and construct a poem in my head
that could encompass my day.

BUTTERFLIES

I feel like an Olympic swimmer in a kiddie pool, not obtaining my full potential due to limiting circumstances. My past, containing abuse and lies, clouds my current mindset with fear and distrust.
I obtain the inability to see a future with someone, no matter the physical attraction.
You unexpectedly came along.
I have always been told that people like you appear, have patience. I have been patient, my prayers have been answered.
I remembered you from your array of distinctive tattoos that interested me enough to muster up the courage to ask about. We had an instant connection, but with my flippant emotions, this was nothing novel.
You said some phrases that made my heart skip a couple beats or a few minutes worth. The conversation ended, I cease to remember how due to my euphoria from multiple sources. A month went by, you were obsolete to my mind, and I considered it a loss. Second month and you had placed the ball back in my court for me to volley.
I took the opportunity that was you and ran with it.
Love does not start off slow when the time is against you, and you trust too quickly, it sprints.
We talked through every hour the opposing time zones would allow. Every moment shared with you made it obvious the direction we were headed.
You captured my heart, it is backpacking through Europe.

RX

I am sick with an illness a specialist can not treat.

Nausea
Slight dizziness
Cluttered thoughts
Rapid heart rate
Lack of focus
Fluttering eyes
Extreme amounts of energy

There is no cure for the only sickness I enjoy obtaining.
When I first saw your smile, you must have been
contagious.
I contracted that loving look and have felt wicked since.
You cause my head to spin and my heart to race every
time your eyes gaze into mine.
My life expectancy is low, but my decaying immaturity
will not be missed.

SOBERLY HALLUCINATING

I obtain this vision of an augmented reality where you
and I travel, budgetless, yet broke.
Imagine waking up next to me, it is 10am in Italy but
4am in America.
We are free to answer or ignore anyone we wish.
It feels like an ecstasy, it feels like adolescence.
Our days filled with adventures and our nights brimming
with spontaneity.
We arise every morning with a mountain to climb or a
city to explore.
The climb is extended, but my love for you stretches
further.
The city is bountiful of luxury, but you already provide
everything I necessitate.
We fell for each other as quickly as our limiting
schedules allowed.
I would do anything with you.
I would do anything for you.
I wish I were eating a pastry with you in Italy.
I wish we were as psychically close as we are mentally.
I dream of exploring foreign places with you while you
review for your international studies class.
We could be five thousand miles overseas; instead,
limitations cause our divide.

LET ME GET MY THOUGHTS STRAIGHT

I want to feel your strawberry hair glide in between my
fingertips as I gaze into your bright eyes.
Reading behind one's glazed pupils is a specialty of
mine, yours tell me you want me forever.
The last time someone's glare expressed this emotion, he
eventually destroyed my ability to love.
He had that same look as you do.
The difference is you are selfless, and he is a narcissist.
I need to stop comparing a hopeful future to an abusive
past.

FOR THE LAST TIME

How unfortunate,
a taste of your own bitter manipulation!
I will sit back and enjoy every single day without your
abuse,
as you sulk over the loss of my affection.
In your own doing,
you placed the cards in my hand,
and I played them as precisely you played me last time I
invested in you.
How does it feel to experience the same grief
that ruined weeks for me?
Is it not so fun to sit around
and fantasize
about the one who defaced your worth, is it?

ONE MORE TIME

How unfortunate,
I continue to lie to myself!
I will sit back and create a facade that I do not withhold
tears
due to your absence.
In your own doing,
you forced me to love you so much
that I had to be rid of you.
It feels agonizing to know
you rarely reminisce about me.
It is not fun to lay in bed,
forcing my pillow to act as a sponge
for my tears wept over the loss of your novelty.

TUESDAY

Separated not by distance,
but by a tax bracket, our love is unobtainable.
I feel as if we would have had potential in a world
where a monetary system did not affect attraction.
Personally, the affection you provided through actions
was more valuable than any dollar sign amount that
could ever provide.
You rebuilt my self-image from rock bottom
as quickly as you tore it down.
Now, you have become a contact
that I avoid clicking in my phone.
The two initials that I correlate to a time
where I wished for something so implausible.

I DREAMT FOR ONCE TONIGHT, AND YOU WERE IN IT

I can envision him sitting in the empty seat
next to me.
20,000 feet up,
holding my hand,
or it on my inner leg.
Passports tucked away,
a little bit of money.
We saved for a spring jailbreak,
this feels like bliss.
This feels so beautiful that it is smooth
like porcelain and polished like gold.
We land and grab a car.
We are touring the world with
pushpins and map in pocket,
pressing holes into every city we explore.
We do not need money,
we do not want money actually.
We want our company
and a bus pass when we land.
He wants to document it all,
I want to collect small moments in time to
save them in a bottle.
We truly never leave home,
considering he is my home,
and I am his.

58 MINUTES IN THE AIR

Crying in seat 11B
of an arbitrary airline
with my passport resting in my lap,
because I have come to the conclusion
that there is no place in the world
where I am
content
happy
and
comfortable.
So I sit in seat 11B
of an arbitrary airline,
flying home to my life
filled with
humidity
routine
and frustration.
So I can arrange another trip
to leave the country
in search of something I will never find.

NOVEMBER, 2017

I have not showered in a couple days.
All I can stomach is the heel of a loaf of bread I
scavenge for at midnight.
I have been drinking mostly water,
or that is what it is beginning to taste like.
My mouth tastes like my own again.
My psychologist resides in the songs
I play to remind myself I am still alive.
It is only going to get harder,
it is impossible for the pain to decay.
I am a psychopath locked up in
solitary confinement that is my mind.
A scream would aid the pressure,
but unfortunately, that would
attract the attention I want.
Stay quiet for now,
or six months.

-me too

TO MY THREE DEADLIEST SINS

Thank you for abandoning me in my darkest moments
out of
<u>Spite</u>
<u>Hurt</u>
<u>Revenge</u>
I cry at the absence of the conversation provided
<u>At 7am</u>
<u>Anytime</u>
<u>Midnight</u>
I feel like a piece of my personality is missing because
of the similarities we obtained with
<u>Knowledge</u>
<u>Music</u>
<u>Hurt</u>
Thank you for leaving me when
<u>I felt closest to you</u>
<u>I hoped things were normal</u>
<u>I wanted more</u>
Because of you, I can not
<u>Laugh</u>
<u>Trust</u>
<u>Love</u>
Because of you, I can
<u>Write</u>
<u>Dance</u>
<u>Inspire</u>

ABOUT THE AUTHOR

Shockey Sanders, is a seventeen-year old poet from a small beach town in south Florida. Sanders became interested in poetry after winning a contest in fourth grade with a poem about Christmas gifts. The prize for the contest was writing lessons that Sanders became fond of after the first session. She fell in love with the art and freedom of words and short stories. After school, she would rush home to fill blank journals with stories and ideas. When she hit high school, she found more mature and relatable topics to expel on the pages. What truly pushed Sanders to make poetry a

full-time hobby, was her first heartbreak and the coping that came along with it. She found that releasing her internalized emotions unto notes on her phone became a healthy form of therapy. Ever since her first experience with adolescent love, Sanders was inspired to write *Under The Impression* about those who have walked in and out of her life.

26403314R00041

Made in the USA
Columbia, SC
09 September 2018